Pet Crazy

Also by
Vardell & Wong

Here We Go:
A Poetry Friday Power Book
A CBC Hot Off the Press Selection

You Just Wait:
A Poetry Friday Power Book
An NCTE Poetry Notable

The Poetry Friday Anthology (K–5)
A Children's Poet Laureate Pick of the Month

The Poetry Friday Anthology for Middle School
An NCTE Poetry Notable
A Children's Poet Laureate Pick of the Month

The Poetry Friday Anthology for Science
NSTA Recommends
A Children's Poet Laureate Pick of the Month

The Poetry Friday Anthology for Celebrations
An ILA Notable Book for a Global Society

PET CRAZY

A Poetry Friday Power Book

12 PowerPlay Prewriting Activities
+12 Anchor Poems
+12 Response Poems
+12 Mentor Poems
+12 Power2You Writing Prompts
+12 Resource Lists for Young Writers & Pet People
with Hidden Language Skills

by
Sylvia Vardell & Janet Wong

illustrations by
Franzi Paetzold

Pomelo Books

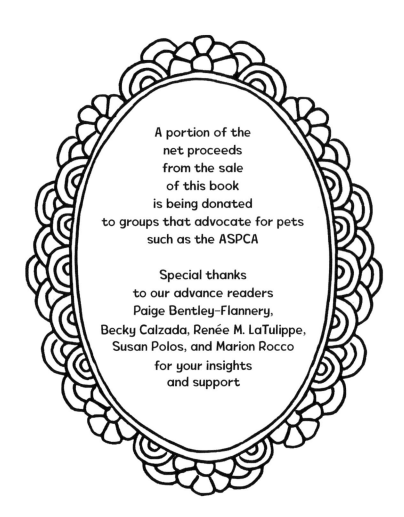

A portion of the
net proceeds
from the sale
of this book
is being donated
to groups that advocate for pets
such as the ASPCA

Special thanks
to our advance readers
Paige Bentley-Flannery,
Becky Calzada, Renée M. LaTulippe,
Susan Polos, and Marion Rocco
for your insights
and support

Pomelo Books
4580 Province Line Road
Princeton, NJ 08540
PomeloBooks.com
info@PomeloBooks.com

The Poetry Friday Anthology® is a registered trademark of Pomelo Books. Library of Congress Cataloging-in-Publication Data is available.
ISBN 978-1-937057-71-8

Please visit us:
PomeloBooks.com

A POETRY FRIDAY POWER BOOK: A NOTE FOR TEACHERS AND PARENTS

Why is this a "Poetry Friday Power Book"? Because we believe poetry helps us express our deepest feelings and our most powerful experiences, and inspires us to use our words to share our thoughts. Plus, we want children to discover the **power** of poetry in their own thinking and writing. They can try these PowerPlay prewriting activities and Power2You writing prompts that pull them into poetry and inspire them to get their own ideas on paper—right now in this book.

And why "Poetry Friday"? Because we found our inspiration for this book in the 700+ poems from *The Poetry Friday Anthology*® series. We used these and other new poems as the starting point for a story about the special place that our pets have in our lives—adding 24 new poems written by Janet Wong that tie the whole story-in-poems together.

This is an example of what children can do when they read, gather, and collect their favorite poems from other books or magazines. Children may enjoy making connections between poems by many different poets, on many different topics, and from many different places. They can create characters and write their own poems to weave those favorite poems together in a story only they can tell.

This book offers several choices for reading, thinking, writing, and responding. Overall, it's a story in poems, but all of this is also organized in PowerPack groups that help children get a "behind the scenes" look at how poems work and how poets write and think. In each of these PowerPack groups, you'll find five things:

- PowerPlay Prewriting Activity
- Anchor Poem (from an outside source)
- Response Poem
- Mentor Poem
- Power2You Writing Prompt

Children can have fun reading and thinking about poetry and learning about how poetry uses just a few words, but says so much and can inspire us to share our own thoughts and feelings. In addition, there are "Hidden Language Skills" to discover and explore, all detailed on pages 114-115. Ready? Let's "power up" and get started!

TABLE OF CONTENTS

Here is a list of the poems that anchor each cluster or PowerPack of activities, response poems, mentor poems, and writing prompts, along with other components that make this book interactive.

POWERPACK 1

PowerPlay Activity

Mix and Match

Anchor Poem

"All Worn Out" by Kristy Dempsey

Response Poem

"Kristy: The Greatest Pets Ever" by Janet Wong

Mentor Poem

"Ben: The Perfect Pets for Me" by Janet Wong

Power2You Writing Prompt

The Perfect Pets for Me (a poem with rhyme)

Mix and Match

Some poets use rhyme at the end of lines or even in the middle. Here are some words that rhyme. Draw a line connecting each pair of rhyming words.

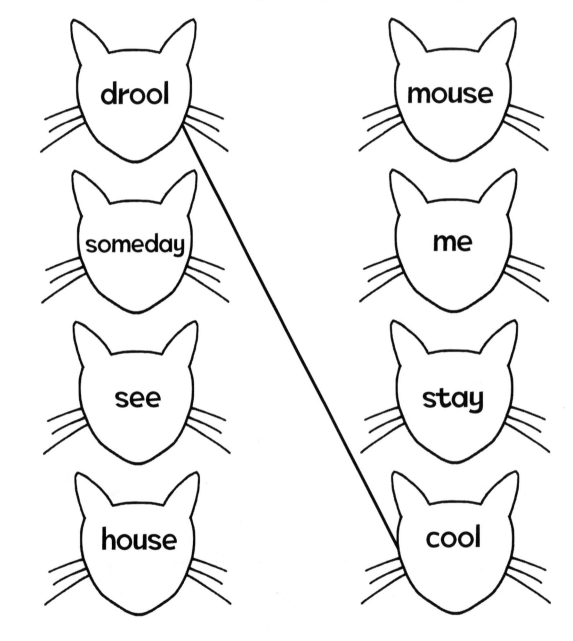

Draw a line connecting each pair of rhyming words here too.

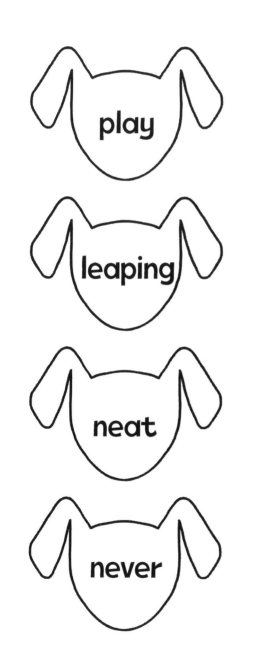

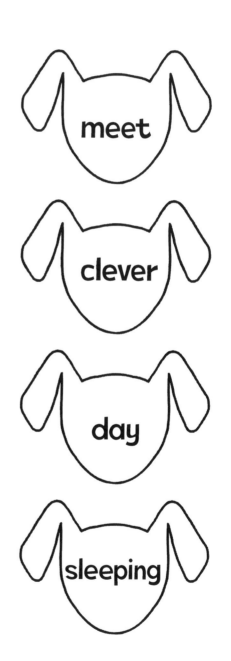

play

meet

leaping

clever

neat

day

never

sleeping

All Worn Out
by Kristy Dempsey

Tippy-toe, Kitty Cat
is sneaking through the house,
pushing on a puff of yarn,
wishing for a mouse.
Kitty loves to play all day,
jumping, pouncing, leaping.
Where is kitty hiding now?
Shh! Kitty's sleeping.

Kristy

The Greatest Pets Ever

Cats are

the greatest pets ever!

They are

so clean and clever.

Would I like

a dog? No, never!

Cats are

my favorites—FOREVER!

Ben
The Perfect Pets for Me

Kristy likes neat pets.
Cats don't drool.

She should meet my uncle's dogs.
They're super-cool.

My uncle's dogs will sit and stay—
and stay and s-t-a-y.

Their house is kind of far,
but we could go there someday.

When we play together,
Kristy will see:

dogs are pretty much
the perfect pets for me!

The Perfect Pets for Me
(a poem with rhyme)

Try writing a poem of your own that uses **rhyme** at the ends of lines. You can write about a pet of your own, a pet you would like to have, whether you prefer cats or dogs, or another topic that interests you.

15

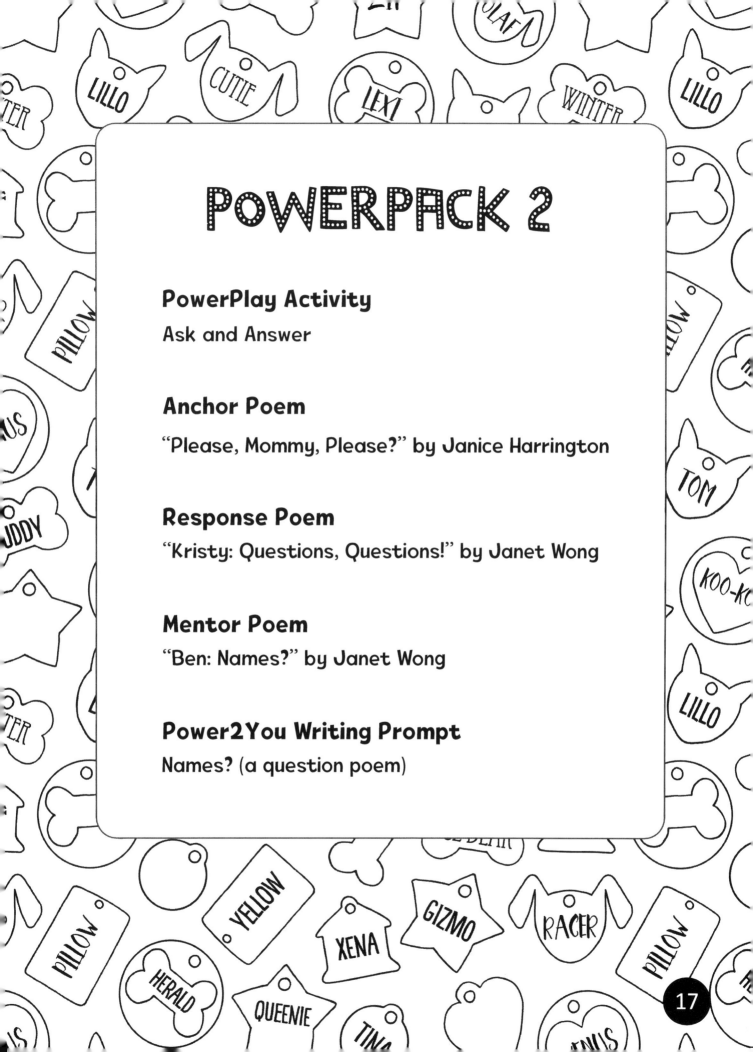

POWERPACK 2

PowerPlay Activity

Ask and Answer

Anchor Poem

"Please, Mommy, Please?" by Janice Harrington

Response Poem

"Kristy: Questions, Questions!" by Janet Wong

Mentor Poem

"Ben: Names?" by Janet Wong

Power2You Writing Prompt

Names? (a question poem)

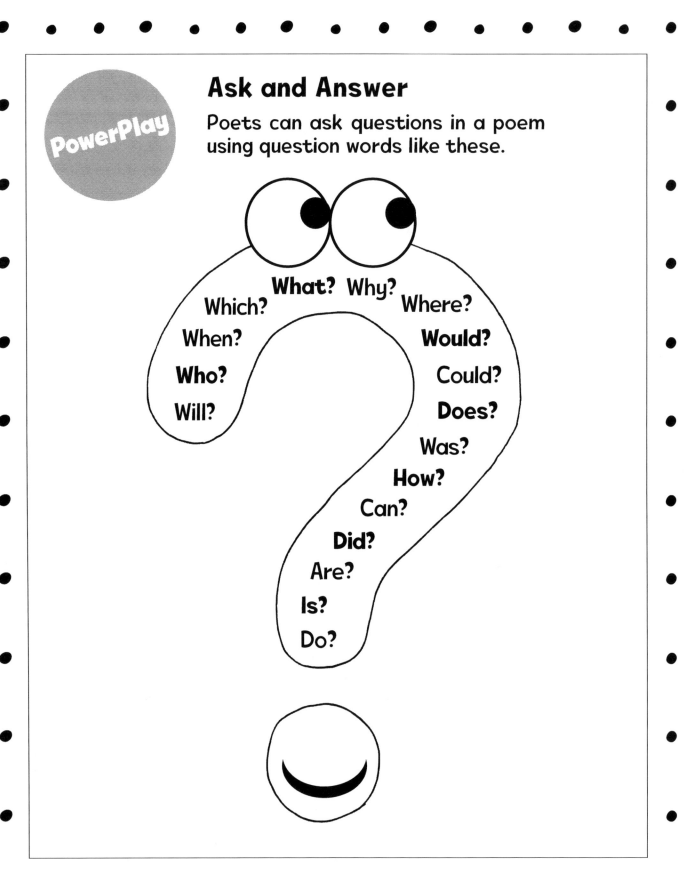

Ask and Answer

Poets can ask questions in a poem using question words like these.

What? Why?
Which? Where?
When? **Would?**
Who? Could?
Will? **Does?**
Was?
How?
Can?
Did?
Are?
Is?
Do?

Questions must end with a question mark. Color the correct ending punctuation that fits each example below.

Where is my lizard   (.) (?)

My kitten likes milk   (.) (?)

Do you have a dog   (.) (?)

Could we get a cat   (.) (?)

That puppy is hungry   (.) (?)

Who is coming today   (.) (?)

Are you ready for a pet   (.) (?)

We need to get dog food   (.) (?)

Please, Mommy, Please?
by Janice Harrington

All I want is a puppy, I say.

Please, Mommy, please?

A puppy who wants to play.

Please, Mommy, please?

A large one, a small one,

a fat one, a tall one—

any puppy is okay.

Please, Mommy, please?

I'll clean up after it and train it too.

I'll teach it what good dogs do.

I'll never let it run away.

Please, Mommy, please?

Kristy
Questions, Questions!

Even before you get a pet,
there's a lot to think about.

Big like a Boxer?
Tiny as a toy?

Choose a girl?
Adopt a boy?

What will you name it?
What happens when you're gone?

The list of questions
goes on and on!

Ben

Names?

Angel, Buddy, Cookie, Duff.

Eagle, Finny, Gus-Gus, Huff.

Ice-bear. Jam-bear.

Koo-koo? Lily?

Monster!

Nothing!

Olaf. Pretty.

Queenie, Racer, Summer, Tina.

Ugly?

Venus, Winter, Xena.

I like Yellow.

Zip sounds fun!

Maybe just

Pet #1?

Names

(a question poem)

Try writing a poem that uses a **question**. You can use questions from these poems or another question you have. You can place it anywhere you like in your poem. Your poem does not need to have an answer to your question either.

23

POWERPACK 3

PowerPlay Activity

Words, Words, Words

Anchor Poem

"Loose Tooth, Whose Tooth?"
                    by Carole Boston Weatherford

Response Poem

"Daniel: On My Hike" by Janet Wong

Mentor Poem

"Ben: My Birthday Is Coming!" by Janet Wong

Power2You Writing Prompt

My Birthday Is Coming! (a poem with repetition)

Words, Words, Words

Words are the building blocks of poems. These words come from the poems in this book. Circle your favorite words or cross out those you don't like.

cat	snake	go
house	wings	outside
wish	lizard	smile
mouse	presents	happy
play	birthday	wonder
jump	frogs	tail
hide	mice	share
sleep	rabbit	words
pets	crickets	book
dog	fish	friends
perfect	horses	lost
puppy	turtles	meow
kitten	parrots	strange

walk	trouble	speak
love	vet	like
feelings	help	ask
share	promise	best
wiggle	family	feed
box	hug	fine
clever	kind	myself
eat	thank	please
world	whistle	see
free	snack	time
keep	lonely	tickle
leap	leash	wander
stop	question	tooth
me	cookies	bugs
rock	adopt	surprise
scratch	gift	think
yarn	no	wiggle
home	show	stay

Loose Tooth, Whose Tooth?
by Carole Boston Weatherford

Loose tooth, whose tooth?

Bat's tooth, rat's tooth.

Loose tooth, whose tooth?

Snail's tooth, whale's tooth.

Loose tooth, whose tooth?

Aardvark's tooth, shark's tooth.

Loose tooth, whose tooth?

Shrew's tooth, gnu's tooth.

Loose tooth, whose tooth?

Gorilla's tooth, chinchilla's tooth.

Loose tooth, whose tooth?

Piranha's tooth, iguana's tooth.

Loose tooth, whose tooth?

Boar's tooth, your tooth.

Daniel
On My Hike

On my hike today
I found a really sharp tooth.
I yelped when I touched it.
That's the truth!

And I caught a lizard
for my best friend Ben.
I'll keep it in a box
until his birthday, then

I'll bring it to his house.
Will his mom let him keep it?
It's going to be hard
to keep this secret!

Ben
My Birthday Is Coming!

My birthday is coming!
I'm getting a surprise.

I can definitely see it
in my parents' eyes.

I heard my mother whispering
"present" to Daniel.

My birthday is coming!
Will my present be a . . .

spaniel?

My Birthday Is Coming!

(a poem with repetition)

Try writing a poem that uses **repetition**. You can repeat a phrase or a line more than once like "I found" or "My birthday is coming!" You might write about a pet, a hobby, a special birthday, or something else.

POWERPACK 4

PowerPlay Activity

Two By Two

Anchor Poem

"Pet Week Show-and-Tell" by Eric Ode

Response Poem

"Ben: Wishing for a Pet" by Janet Wong

Mentor Poem

"Daniel: The Best Gift Yet?" by Janet Wong

Power2You Writing Prompt

The Best Gift Yet? (a poem in stanzas)

PowerPlay

Two By Two

Sometimes poems are arranged in groups of lines called stanzas. And sometimes they rhyme too. Here are examples of stanzas of two lines that rhyme. YOU decide how each one ends.

Choose **one** of these words:

bin violin pin win grin spin

If I had a _____ twin _____

we might share a _____ .

Choose **one** of these words:

alphabet   jet   net   pet

Everybody needs at least one _____ .

Choose **one** of these words:

sunset   vet

Have you seen a _____ yet?

Choose **ONE** column. Then choose **TWO** words from that column and use them to finish the sentences below.

stick	cake	call	hop
tick	lake	fall	pop
click	rake	hall	shop
trick	fake	ball	mop
kick	shake	wall	laptop
pick	brake	mall	stop
brick	snake	stall	top

I wish I had a _____ .

But I don't want a _____ .

Pet Week Show-and-Tell
by Eric Ode

Pet Week! Pet Week!

Frogs croak, mice squeak.

Rabbits hop, snakes hiss.

Crickets chirp, fish kiss.

Dogs howl, horses neigh.

Turtles crawl, kittens play.

Lizards scurry, parrots speak.

Hurry! Hurry! Pet Week!

Ben
Wishing for a Pet

Kristy brought pictures of her cat
with its favorite old toy mouse.

Daniel brought a nestbox.
It's a wooden bluebird house.

Robert brought a rabbit.
Sophia brought a fish.

What did I bring? Nothing—
but I'll share my birthday wish!

Daniel
The Best Gift Yet?

Ben's birthday party
starts in a minute.

And this fancy box has . . .
a lizard in it!

The Best Gift Yet?

(a poem in stanzas)

Try writing a poem with **stanzas.** You can organize your poem with one-line, two-line, or four-line stanzas, or a mix of these. You can focus on a pet, a birthday, a surprise, or another topic of your choice.

POWERPACK 5

PowerPlay Activity

All Smiles

Anchor Poem

"Disappointed" by Helen Frost

Response Poem

"Daniel: Real Feelings" by Janet Wong

Mentor Poem

"Daniel: I'm Sorry" by Janet Wong

Power2You Writing Prompt

I'm Sorry (a poem expressing emotion)

All Smiles

Poets often express their emotions in the poems they write. They can feel sad, happy, or excited, or even make you laugh. Think about how you feel at different times.

Draw the emoji face that shows how you feel in each of these situations.

I feel ◯ when I see a

I feel ◯ when I read

I feel ◯ when you

I feel ◯ when I play

I feel ◯ when I eat

I feel ◯ when I get a

Disappointed
by Helen Frost

I wanted a pet

I could talk to.

Someone to take for a walk.

A dog or cat

that would love me—

not this lizard that sits on a rock.

I toss in some crickets.

It catches and eats them,

and that's about it for the day.

Was I asking too much

for my birthday this year?

I wanted a pet that could play.

Daniel
Real Feelings

Ben tried
so hard to show
he thought
the lizard was fun.

He watched it
for a minute or two
and even fed
a few bugs to it.

You could see
his real feelings, though.

Should I let the lizard go?

Daniel

I'm Sorry

We took the box outside
and tipped it gently
on the lawn.

Poof!
Shazam!

The lizard was gone!

Ben's smile was back again.
And I felt happy, too.

I'm sorry, Lizard,
that we bothered you!

I'm Sorry

(a poem expressing emotion)

Try writing a poem that **expresses your feelings** about something important to you. These can be happy feelings of joy, sad feelings about something difficult, or feelings of worry or surprise.

47

POWERPACK 6

PowerPlay Activity

Double Time

Anchor Poem

"New Idea" by Tamera Will Wissinger

Response Poem

"Ben: Bouncing Along the Trail" by Janet Wong

Mentor Poem

"Daniel: A Weekend Away" by Janet Wong

Power2You Writing Prompt

A Weekend Away (a poem with alliteration)

PowerPlay

Double Time

Sometimes poets use words for the special sounds they make. They even use many words that start with the same sound. Finish each of these examples with words that begin with the same sound as each name.

Olivia likes <u>oceans</u> .

Ben likes   b _____ .

Daniel likes d _____ .

Tommy likes t _____ .

Alex likes a _____ .

Maria likes m _____ .

Noah likes n _____ .

Emily likes e _____ .

Now finish each of these examples with action words. What could each of these characters DO? Think of an action word that begins with the same letter as each name.

Cara <u>climbs</u> .

Hailey h_____ .

Johnny j_____ .

Paul p_____ .

Robert r_____ .

Lee l_____ .

Will w_____ .

Sofia s_____ .

New Idea
by Tamera Will Wissinger

Wandering, wandering through the woods,
Uncle Jesse, three dogs, and me.

Wondering, wondering why we're here—
a haze hides most of the trees.

Whistling, whistling, uncle calls.
Dogs gather, their tails thump the ground.

Libby leaps. Sal stays and scratches her scruff.
Barnaby turns around.

Sal brings a stick. I grab hold, throw it long.
Sky and sun show through fog.

Welcoming, welcoming new idea:
my uncle is sharing his dogs.

Ben
Bouncing Along the Trail

Uncle Jesse jokes:
"Just
took ten minutes
walking with
the dogs
to perk you up."

It's funny
that they wonder
why
I want a pup!

Daniel
A Weekend Away

Grandpa and I
(and his dog Ruby)
went camping together
last week.

We built big fires
and melted marshmallows.
Ruby played fetch
by the creek.

Grandpa caught five fish—
not bad.
But guess what?
I caught seven!

What a wild weekend—
so fun!
I think
it was holiday heaven!

A Weekend Away

(a poem with alliteration)

Try writing a poem that uses several words that begin with the same letter. This is a special sound effect called **alliteration.** You can focus on a special time with family or a pet or another topic of your choice.

POWERPACK 7

PowerPlay Activity
First Things First

Anchor Poem
"Book Hound" by Elizabeth Steinglass

Response Poem
"Kristy: READING" by Janet Wong

Mentor Poem
"Daniel: WRITING" by Janet Wong

Power2You Writing Prompt
WRITING (an acrostic poem)

First Things First

Sometimes poets use a key word to focus the topic of their poems—for example, READING. See if you can think of 2 or 3 words that begin with each of the following letters. You can choose words from the list on the next page or use words of your own.

R is for   ran   ride   round

E is for _____

A is for _____

D is for _____

I is for _____

N is for _____

G is for _____

about	do	good
after	does	got
again	don't	green
all	done	grow
always	draw	if
am	drink	into
an	eat	its
any	eight	never
are	every	new
around	gave	no
as	get	ran
ask	give	read
at	giving	ride
ate	goes	right
did	now	round

Book Hound
by Elizabeth Steinglass

Ruby settles next to me,

Ears up, eyes twinkling,

Asking without words

Do you have a book?

I show her the cover.

Nice, she wriggles.

Go on, she nudges, so I

Begin turning shapes into sounds,

Uncovering a new world,

Discovering new friends.

Did you like it? I ask at the end.

Yes, she yips. Again! Again!

Kristy
READING

Reading out loud to a rabbit?

Everybody giggles when they hear

About it for the first time. But when they

Do it, they discover how much fun

It is. Our Reading Rabbit at school

Never cares if I make a mistake. I just

Grab a book and read!

Daniel
WRITING

When I read to our

Reading Rabbit, my

Imagination gets hopping—

That's the best time to write.

I have filled a whole

Notebook with great ideas I

Got from books!

WRITING

(an acrostic poem)

Try writing a special poem called an **acrostic poem.**
In an acrostic poem, the first letter of each line
spells a key word (like READING). You can write about
a special animal, a school experience, a favorite
book, or something else that interests you.

POWERPACK 8

PowerPlay Activity

Lost and Found

Anchor Poem

"Lost and Found" by Laura Shovan

Response Poem

"Kristy: Cat Song" by Janet Wong

Mentor Poem

"Kristy: Sick" by Janet Wong

Power2You Writing Prompt

Sick (a found poem)

Lost and Found

You can find a powerful word or a great idea in many places once you start looking. Start by finding the lost cat in the maze below.

Now hunt for the sentence hidden in the CIRCLES in the maze below. Write the letter you find in each circle ◯ on the lines below the maze.

START

R

f
i n d
l
s S a x
c e h t
k b 4
2
j g c
p
w v o r z
5 9 8 e m

END

_____ ____ ___

Lost and Found (a found poem)
by Laura Shovan

I'm a **curious** cat.

My gray tail twitches.

I **chase bird** shadows

from lawn to lawn.

When I've **lost**

the scent of **home**,

I cry a sad song.

Meow! Meow!

Someone **find** me.

See my **collar?**

Call that number.

Take me **home.**

Based on this text:

Each year, thousands of pets get lost. Some of them get lost while they chase birds or squirrels. Some of them wander away from home because they are curious about something. When they finally look up, they discover that they are lost. Putting a pet license tag on your pet's collar—and keeping the collar on at all times—is the best way to make sure that someone can find your pet and return it to you.

Kristy
Cat Song

M e o w!
M e o w!

My song:
I'm home!

Based on this text:

Lost and Found (a found poem)
by Laura Shovan

I'm a curious cat.
My gray tail twitches.
I chase bird shadows
from lawn to lawn.
When I've lost
the scent of home,
I cry a sad song.
Meow! Meow!
Someone find me.
See my collar?
Call that number.
Take me home.

Kristy
Sick (a found poem)

Gaining weight quickly? CHECK!

Strange behavior? CHECK!

Sluggish and tired? CHECK!

Trouble getting up? CHECK!

Strange lumps? CHECK!

What is my conclusion?

Time to go to the VET!

Based on this text:

From the website of the U.S. National Library of Medicine, https://medlineplus.gov/pethealth.html:

Pets can add fun, companionship and a feeling of safety to your life. Before getting a pet, think carefully about which animal is best for your family. What is each family member looking for in a pet? Who will take care of it? Does anyone have pet allergies? What type of animal suits your lifestyle and budget?

Once you own a pet, keep it healthy. Know the signs of medical problems. Take your pet to the veterinarian if you notice:

- Loss of appetite
- Drinking a lot of water
- Gaining or losing a lot of weight quickly
- Strange behavior
- Being sluggish and tired
- Trouble getting up or down
- Strange lumps

Sick

(a found poem)

Try writing a **found** poem of your own. Look for words from another source (like the pages of this book). Choose those words, add more words of your own, and arrange them all into a poem. You can write about an animal or pet or another subject that interests you.

POWERPACK 9

PowerPlay Activity
Time to Talk

Anchor Poem
"Trust" by Padma Venkatraman

Response Poem
"Kristy: Our Vet Speaks Cat" by Janet Wong

Mentor Poem
"Ben: Good News!" by Janet Wong

Power2You Writing Prompt
Good News! (a dialogue poem)

Time to Talk

Sometimes poems sound like people talking to one another. Imagine what these characters might say to each other and write those words in the speech balloons. Here's an example:

Trust
by Padma Venkatraman

My cat
hissed and spat
at the vet. "I'll help,"
I said. She squirmed and yelped
when I held her tight.

To calm her fright
I kissed her head
and whispered soothing words.

She
licked me
with her ticklish tongue.

Her grass-green eyes
gazed into mine.
"You'll be fine,"
I promised,

feeling like my mommy
must have felt,
holding squalling baby
me,
when we visited a doctor.

Kristy
Our Vet Speaks Cat

Our vet is speaking "Cat"
to our cat—
with her eyes,
with her hums,
with her hands.

And our cat is speaking "Vet"
right back—
with her whiskers,
with her fur,
with her purrs.

Our vet and our cat
understand each other,
but to me it sounds like
    "Hmm, hummm"
        "rrrrr, purrrrrr" . . .

I guess a big part
of becoming a vet
is learning to speak
all kinds of "Pet"!

Ben
Good News!

Me: "Kristy's cat is sick."

Mom: "That's part of having a pet."

Me: "Is Kristy's cat going to die?"

Mom: "Let's see what they hear
from the vet."

Phone: Ring! Rringg!!

Mom: "What did you say?
That's great! That's crazy!"

Me: "Kristy's cat isn't sick?"

Mom: "She's just having babies!"

Good News!

(a dialogue poem)

Try writing a poem with **dialogue** in it. Include words or lines spoken between two or more characters (and be sure to use quotation marks correctly). You can write about your family, a pet, or another topic.

POWERPACK 10

PowerPlay Activity

Word Finder

Anchor Poem

"How to Love Your Little Corner of the World"
by Eileen Spinelli

Response Poem

"Kristy: I Need Help!" by Janet Wong

Mentor Poem

"Ben: Helping Our Neighbors" by Janet Wong

Power2You Writing Prompt

Helping Our Neighbors (a list poem)

Word Finder

Poets choose each word for their poems very carefully, hunting for just the right word. Your turn! Hunt for 17 words from the poems in this book hidden in the puzzle below (going across or up and down).

h e l p d b p e t s
u t a l k o w d o g
g f c a t o r n o f
w r w a l k q i d e
e e f r i e n d a e
e e s p i l l m y d
k t r e e s e v e n

Search for these words:

help   tree   hug   pets   cat   dog   book   talk   no
feed   free   walk   my   week   seven   friend   spill   day

Make your own word search. Choose 5 or 6 words from the poems in this book and insert the letters for each word in the box below, going across or up and down. Fill any empty spaces with any additional letters you choose. Share with a friend.

```
r           n  x  p  c  e  k
l  q  c  i  h  d  c  m  i  d
n     v  k  f
g     s  x     n  p  w  q  j
h     a  t     v  j  k  s
p     i  w     r  y  m  z
u  d  m                    a
```

Search for these words: (Write the words you choose to add to the puzzle here.)

How to Love Your Little Corner of the World

by Eileen Spinelli

Help a neighbor.

Plant a tree.

Hug your friends

and family.

Be kind to pets.

Feed the birds.

Use your please

and thank you words.

Share a book.

Take a walk.

Someone's lonely?

Stop and talk.

Kristy
I Need Help!

The kittens are here!
Three of them . . . a trio
of *tumblestorms!*
I need help:

> wiping spills,
>
> filling bowls,
>
> cleaning puddles,
>
> washing towels.

> Catching kittens on the loose,
>
> saying "no!"
>
> and "no!" and "no!"
>
> every time they
>
> scratch or
>
> bite.

Would you like a free kitten
tonight?

Ben
Helping Our Neighbors

People used to call me Ben.
But now they call me
the "Dog-Walker Kid."

I walk seven dogs
to help our neighbors.
There is one dog
for each day of the week.

Monday: Monster
Tuesday: Tina
Wednesday: Winter
Thursday: Thunder
Friday: Fred
Saturday: Sammy
Sunday: Summer

I have seven dogs.
And seven dogs have me!

Helping Our Neighbors

(a list poem)

Try writing a **list** poem about a pet, a hobby, or advice for the reader. Your whole poem can be a list or just a part of your poem can be a list of items or ideas.

POWERPACK 11

PowerPlay Activity

Draw the Line

Anchor Poem

"I Had to Get a Shot at the Doctor's"
                                by April Halprin Wayland

Response Poem

"Ben: My Newest Friend" by Janet Wong

Mentor Poem

"Kristy: Homes" by Janet Wong

Power2You Writing Prompt

Homes (a free verse poem)

Draw the Line

Sometimes it helps to draw before you write. We can draw, doodle, or scribble and begin to get ideas about what to write about. For some people drawing is easy, but sometimes we need help. Here are easy steps for drawing a cat.

Follow the steps and draw a cat (or cats). Think about giving your cat a name or writing a poem about your cat.

I Had to Get a Shot at the Doctor's
by April Halprin Wayland

and my arm hurt

and it still hurts as we get to the dog park

and James and his dogs show up

and we all spill through the double gate

and our red, green and blue leashes tangle

and I am laughing because we are so tangled

and our dogs are so goofy

and now it doesn't hurt.

Ben

My Newest Friend

Last week at Washington Avenue Park
I made a new friend, James,
who has a Boston terrier named Bossy
and a Great Dane named G.D.

James just moved here
from North Dakota.
He lives on the same street
as my friend Kristy.

Kristy invited me and Daniel
and James and his sister, Amy,
over for a snack today.
We had cookies and milk
while playing with her kittens.

Maybe cats aren't so bad
after all?

Kristy

Homes

We're keeping one kitten—
plus our mommy cat, Sweetness.
We need two good homes for the others.

Today while we ate cookies,
Amy played with the littlest kitten.
She laughed
when he wiggled his whiskers
and chased his tail.
I asked, "Would you like to adopt him?"
Amy shouted, "YES!"

When Amy's mom came,
Amy whispered in her ear.
Her mom nodded.
Sweetness licked her littlest kitten
and then licked Amy.

One more home to go!

Homes

(a free verse poem)

Try writing a poem with no rhyme or rules. You can still have a strong rhythm, but the ends of lines should not rhyme. This is called a **free verse** poem. You can write about a favorite pet, a good friend, or another topic.

POWERPACK 12

PowerPlay Activity
Picture That

Anchor Poem
"Kitten" (a rebus poem) by Don Tate

Response Poem
"Ben: Surprise!" (a rebus poem) by Janet Wong

Mentor Poem
"Ben: Pet Crazy" (a rebus poem) by Janet Wong

Power2You Writing Prompt
Pet Crazy (your choice of poem)

Picture That

Poets create pictures in your mind with the words they choose. What pictures do you have in mind when you read the words below? Choose **one** of the following words and draw what you picture in your mind for the meaning of that word.

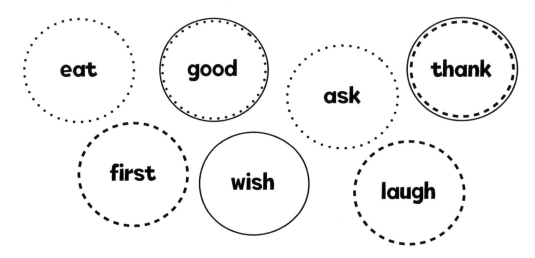

eat   good   ask   thank

first   wish   laugh

Now turn the tables and write a word that goes with each picture below.

Kitten (a rebus poem)
by Don Tate

Got a new  today.

Makes me .

Chases his tail.

 Run – run – run .

Never catches it!

Ben

Surprise! (a rebus poem)

At 🕐 I heard three 👊 .

I opened the 🚪 and found a 🥛 .

What did I see there before my 👀 ?

A very furry little surprise!

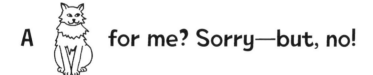

A 🐱 for me? Sorry—but, no!

Kristy, come back—Kristy, don't go!

Ben
Pet Crazy (a rebus poem)

I love my 🐱 but I still want a pup.

I know 1 thing: I won't give ⬆️ !

And after a 🐕 I might get a 🐸 ,

and maybe even two 🐢 too.

I'm PET CRAZY!

How about you?

Pet Crazy

(your choice of poem)

You've experimented with rhyme and repetition. You've tried various poem forms including **question, acrostic, list, found poems,** and **free verse.** You've practiced creating stanzas and using alliteration and dialogue. You've expressed emotions through poetry. Now it's your turn to try writing a poem in any way that you like. You can continue this story, change the ending completely, or write about something totally new. It's up to you!

Love is a four-legged word.

POETRY
FRIDAY
POWER
RESOURCES

WHAT'S NEXT?

In the pages that follow, you'll find all kinds of help for reading and writing more poetry. There's a list of more poems about pets, suggested books of poetry about cats and dogs, and helpful websites about reading to pets. There are tips for sharing poetry out loud and questions to make us think. There is also guidance for helping with writing, recommended books about writing, places to publish, and a list of poetry published by young writers.

We can share our poems during an Open House at school or with friends and family members for a special occasion—or our own private reasons. We can even work as a group to choose favorite poems, write new poems to connect them all into a story, and then perform the story for an audience. Some anthologies that we hope you'll consider first for a project are our books in *The Poetry Friday Anthology* series, which you can learn more about at our website, PomeloBooks.com.

P.S. For an extra challenge, check out the Hidden Language Skills activities on pages 114-115. Here there are instructions for hunting for antonyms, alliteration, onomatopoeia, punctuation, capitalization, special spelling words, number words, vivid vocabulary, and descriptive adjectives. Plus, the answers are there too!

12 MORE POEMS ABOUT PETS FROM THE POETRY FRIDAY ANTHOLOGY® SERIES

The story in this book was built upon poems from The Poetry Friday Anthology® *series, plus new poems written by twelve poets and twenty-four new poems by Janet Wong. Below is a list of MORE poems from* The Poetry Friday Anthology® *series that might be used to start another story.*

PFA = The Poetry Friday Anthology *(K-5 Teacher Edition)*
PFAC = The Poetry Friday Anthology for Celebrations
PFAS = The Poetry Friday Anthology for Science *(or* The Poetry of Science*)*

"Brave Dog!" by Stephanie Calmenson (PFAC)
   *Celebrate guide dogs and other service animals with this poem.

"Dog in a Storm" by Stephanie Calmenson (PFAS)
   *How do pets feel about stormy weather?

"Fish" by Joy Acey (PFA)
   *Thinking about what fish do.

"Goldfish" by Joan Bransfield Graham (PFAMS)
   *Gentle thoughts about a pet burial.

"Jackson" by Libby Martinez (PFAC)
   *Is it possible to know an animal, even if you never speak with each other?

"The Lion and the House Cat" by Mary Lee Hahn (PFAS)
   *Finding similarities in the chin, eyes, stretch, and pride of cats and lions.

"Litter's Littlest" by Avis Harley (PFA)
   *A poem from the point of view of the runt of the litter.

"Mrs. Sepuka's Classroom Pet" by Ken Slesarik (*The Poetry of Science*)
   *Who will take care of the classroom pet during vacation?

"My Pet" by David L. Harrison (PFA)
   *Having a wild "pet" bat (who doesn't know he's your pet).

"Oh Man!" by David L. Harrison (PFA)
   *Wishing for a pet porcupine.

"Petting Zoo" by Laura Purdie Salas (PFA)
   *Meeting goats, bunnies, hogs, dogs, kittens, and a cow.

"Testing My Hypothesis" by Leslie Bulion (PFAS)
   *Do cats love the color red? A home experiment for cats.

POETRY BOOKS ABOUT CATS

Cats have been the subject of poetry around the world, from haiku to classics like "The Owl and the Pussycat." Here is a sampling of "cat" poems of all types. Look for them in the library.

Florian, Douglas. 2003. *Bow Wow Meow Meow: It's Rhyming Cats and Dogs.* San Diego: Harcourt Brace. *Zany, creative poems and paintings that are fun and playful.

Franco, Betsy. 2009. *A Curious Collection of Cats.* San Francisco: Tricycle Press. *This concrete collection features cat poems in various shapes.

Grimes, Nikki. 2007. *When Gorilla Goes Walking.* New York: Orchard Books. *Cecilia shares poems about her cat, Gorilla, and her many interests and talents.

MacLachlan, Patricia and Charest, Emily MacLachlan. 2013. *Cat Talk.* New York: HarperCollins. *Poems from the perspectives of multiple cats with attitude and personality.

Rosen, Michael J. 2015. *The Maine Coon's Haiku and Other Poems for Cat Lovers.* Somerville, MA: Candlewick. *Twenty different cat breeds are featured in vivid poems and illustrations.

Sidman, Joyce. 2006. *Meow Ruff.* Boston: Houghton Mifflin. *An unlikely dog-and-cat friendship develops in poems and concrete visuals.

Wardlaw, Lee. 2011. *Won Ton: A Cat Tale Told in Haiku.* New York: Henry Holt. *A shelter cat gets a new home and a new name, all told in haiku poems.

Wardlaw, Lee. 2015. *Won Ton and Chopstick: A Cat and Dog Tale Told in Haiku.* New York: Henry Holt. *A shelter cat with a new home now has to adjust to a new puppy too.

POETRY BOOKS ABOUT DOGS

Dogs may be "man's best friend," but they've also been the subject of poetry for many years. Here are some of the many poetry books that feature dogs.

Ashman, Linda. 2008. *Stella, Unleashed: Notes from the Doghouse.* New York: Sterling. *This dog has opinions about everything in her life in these funny poems.

Clements, Andrew. 2007. *Dogku.* New York: Simon & Schuster. *A stray pup finds a family and hopes the dad lets him stay, all told in haiku poems.

Franco, Betsy. 2011. A *Dazzling Display of Dogs.* Berkeley, CA: Tricycle. *Here is an assortment of concrete poems about dogs in shapes that suggest their meaning.

George, Kristine O'Connell. 2002. *Little Dog and Duncan.* New York: Clarion. *Two very different dogs form a friendship when one comes to visit the other.

MacLachlan, Patricia and Charest, Emily MacLachlan. 2010. *Once I Ate a Pie.* New York: HarperCollins. *Several different dogs tell their stories in funny, descriptive poems.

Rosen, Michael J. 2011. *The Hound Dog's Haiku and Other Poems for Dog Lovers.* Somerville, MA: Candlewick. *Lively haiku poems about twenty different dog breeds.

Singer, Marilyn, 2012. *Every Day's a Dog's Day: A Year in Poems.* New York: Dial. *A poetic look at different highlights in a year from a dog's point of view.

Sklansky, Amy E. 2002. *From the Doghouse: Poems to Chew On.* New York: Henry Holt. *A fun mix of rhyming poems about puppies, mutts, and dogs of all types.

WEBSITES ABOUT READING TO PETS

Reading to an animal (especially dogs) can be fun and help build confidence and reading skill. Here are a few resources that provide tips and guidelines.

R.E.A.D. Program
The Intermountain Therapy Animals R.E.A.D. (Reading Education Assistance Dog) program is a central resource and has workshops in many places.
TherapyAnimals.org/Read_Affiliate_Programs.html

Tail Waggin' Tutors
Therapy Dogs International has a model program described here.
TDI-dog.org/OurPrograms.aspx?Page=Children+Reading+to+Dogs

SitStayRead.org
This is a program in low-income neighborhoods in Chicago with trained volunteers and Certified Reading Assistance Dogs.

LibraryDogs.com
There are many photos and tips on how to get started and why reading to pets is special.

POETRY WEBSITES YOU NEED TO KNOW

There are many excellent poetry-related websites to explore, with information about poets, sample poems and activities, tips and games, and much more. Here are some of our favorite sites.

Giggle Poetry
GigglePoetry.com
*A fun site with poems plus activities, games, and poem scripts.

No Water River
by Renée M. LaTulippe
NoWaterRiver.com
*Listen to poets read poetry aloud, watch poetry videos, and learn about poetry award winners.

The Poem Farm
by Amy Ludwig VanDerwater
PoemFarm.AmyLV.com
*This poet shares poems as well as her writing process and sound recordings.

Poetry Foundation Children's Page
Poetryfoundation.org/resources/children
*Here are hundreds of poems as well as interesting articles.

Poetry for Kids
by Kenn Nesbitt
Poetry4Kids.com
*A "poetry playground" with funny poems, plus there is a place to sign up to receive a poem a week via email.

The Poetry Minute
PoetryMinute.org
*Poems for every day of the school year.

POETRY PERFORMANCE TIPS

It can be fun to read these poems aloud as a group using simple theater and performance tips.

Simple props can add fun to sharing a poem with a group or larger audience. Use a common object mentioned in the poem as a "poetry prop," and hold it up while reading aloud. For example, bring a leash, pet collar, pet tag, or pet toy to use as a poetry prop when reading these poems aloud.

Adding motions or pantomime while you read a poem aloud can make a poem more engaging. Often it's possible to act out the words of a poem. For example, read aloud "All Worn Out" and add movement for the words *sneaking, jumping, pouncing, leaping,* and *sleeping.*

Poems that have a repeated line or phrase can be fun to read together. For example, "Please, Mommy, Please?" has a repeated line that everyone can chime in on. Or "Loose Tooth, Whose Tooth?" is another example. One person reads most of the poem aloud, but everyone joins in on the repeated line.

Echo reading is another way to read a poem aloud with a group. One person says each line of the poem, pausing after each line so the rest of the group can repeat the line. Poems with short lines work best, like "Pet Week Show-and-Tell" or "All Worn Out" or "Lost and Found."

TALKING POINTS

The activities below can serve as "talking points" to start a discussion about pets—and if anyone has other questions, start with those!

Talk about how it feels to visit the veterinarian or the doctor or the dentist. What helps make a visit easier?

Talk about the dogs and cats you have encountered in your life. If possible, look up images and information about unfamiliar breeds of dogs and cats on the Internet and learn more about them.

In these poems, cats say "Meow," but in other languages, cats make other sounds like "Miaw" (Spanish) or "Nyan" (Japanese). Look at animal sounds in many languages in "Soundimals" by James Chapman at Soundimals.com/#/animals/.

Think about how acts of kindness can come from unexpected places and people. What kindnesses have you noticed and what could you do during Random Acts of Kindness Week or any time?

POETRY WRITING CHECKLIST

Poets of all ages often need help in looking at their own work critically. A checklist can be helpful in learning how to revise and polish our own writing. Here is one example created by poetry teacher Aaren Perry that includes questions that might be helpful. We may not need each step every time. Use the ones that are helpful.

1. What can I put in my poem?
    *Who, what, when, where, why, how?
    *Sight, sound, smell, feel, taste?

2. Maybe I could add
    *More words, more ideas, more feeling?

3. Are there things I would like to fix?
    *Line breaks, spacing?
    *Punctuation, spelling, capitalization?
    *Title, beginning, middle, end?

4. What do I notice when I read it out loud?
    *Does it have a rhythm? Does it rhyme?
    *Is it clear? Is it loud? Quiet? Both?

Based on: Perry, Aaren Yeatts. 1997. "Self-Questioning Guidelines" in *Poetry Across the Curriculum: An Action Guide for Elementary Teachers*. Boston: Allyn & Bacon, p. 183.

BOOKS ABOUT WRITING POETRY

Several poets have written books ABOUT poetry writing. Here are a few that might be helpful.

Kapell, Dave and Steenland, Sally. 1998. *Kids' Magnetic Poetry Book and Creativity Kit*. Workman. *Here are tips and tools for making poetry fun and game-like.

Lawson, JonArno. 2008. *Inside Out: Children's Poets Discuss Their Work*. Walker. *Twenty-three poets share poems and then explain how the poem came to be.

Prelutsky, Jack. 2008. *Pizza, Pigs, and Poetry: How to Write a Poem*. Greenwillow. *The poet shares how he creates poems from anecdotes, often using comic exaggeration.

Salas, Laura Purdie. 2011. *Picture Yourself Writing Poetry: Using Photos to Inspire Writing*. Capstone. *This is a clear and engaging approach with writing prompts and mentor texts.

Meet the Author series
Look for picture books in the "Meet the Author" series. Here, poets like Douglas Florian, Lee Bennett Hopkins, Karla Kuskin, Janet Wong, and Jane Yolen talk about their lives and how they write poetry. These are published by Richard C. Owen Publishers.

PLACES TO PUBLISH YOUR POETRY

Here are several different print and online sources that publish poetry by young writers. Be sure to check the rules before submitting any writing to each place. Give it a try, have fun, and good luck!

Creative Kids
CKmagazine.org
*"This is the nation's largest magazine for and by kids."

New Moon: The Magazine for Girls and Their Dreams
NewMoon.com
*Here is a special online community and magazine for girls.

Skipping Stones
SkippingStones.org
*This is an international, multicultural, environmental magazine.

Stone Soup
StoneSoup.com
*Look for stories, poems, book reviews, and artwork by young people.

BOOKS WITH POEMS BY CHILDREN

Here are several notable books of poetry written by young people.

Lowe, Ayana. Ed. 2008. *Come and Play: Children of Our World Having Fun*. New York: Bloomsbury. *Here are photos of children around the world along with poems by young writers, ages 5-11.

Lyne, Sandford. Ed. 2004. *Soft Hay Will Catch You*. New York: Simon & Schuster. *Kentucky poet Lyne gathers poems by young writers about home and family.

Nye, Naomi Shihab. Ed. 2000. *Salting the Ocean: 100 Poems by Young Poets*. Greenwillow. *Nye collected "100 poems by 100 poets in grades one through twelve."

Rogé. 2014. *Haiti My Country: Poems by Haitian Schoolchildren*. Ill. by Rogé. Fifth House. Markham, Ontario. *Close-up painted portraits of real kids in Haiti accompany their brief personal poems.

Spain, Sahara Sunday. 2001. *If There Would Be No Light: Poems from My Heart*. San Francisco: HarperCollins. *Dig into these poems by a nine-year-old who has traveled the world.

HiDDEN LANGUAGE SKiLLS

*For people who like reading and writing and poetry, it can be fun to take the next step and sharpen our language skills even further. There is a **hidden language skill** in each PowerPack. Look for examples of each of these hidden language skills in the PowerPack poems. The answers are upside down under each PowerPack challenge below.*

PowerPack 1: They're/Their/There

Find the most commonly misspelled and incorrectly used word/s in English—**they're, their,** and **there**—in this poem:

"The Perfect Pets for Me" (p. 14)

They're super-cool.
Their house is kind of far,
but we could go **there** someday.

PowerPack 2: Antonyms

Find pairs of words that mean the opposite of each other in these PowerPack poems:
"Please, Mommy, Please?" (p. 20)
"Questions, Questions!" (p. 21)
"Names?" (p. 22)

"Please, Mommy, Please?"
large/small
"Questions, Questions!"
big/tiny
"Names?"
Pretty/Ugly; Summer/Winter

PowerPack 3: Punctuation

Find the commas (,), question marks (?), apostrophes ('), periods (.), exclamation marks (!), quotation marks (" "), and dots of ellipsis (...).

"Loose Tooth, Whose Tooth?" (p. 28)
There is a comma in EVERY line of this poem. You will also find a question mark ending every other line. Can you find 7 periods and 13 apostrophes in this poem?

"On My Hike" (p. 29)
Can you find the 4 periods, 4 apostrophes, 2 exclamation marks, 1 comma, and 1 question mark in this poem?

"My Birthday Is Coming!" (p. 30)
Find the 1 question mark, 2 exclamation marks, 2 apostrophes, one set of (2) quotation marks, 3 periods, and 3 dots of ellipsis.

PowerPack 4: Its/It's

The words **its** and **it's** are often confused. Find each in the poem **"Wishing for a Pet"** (p. 37).

with **its** favorite old toy mouse.

It's a wooden bluebird house.

PowerPack 5: Onomatopoeia

Can you find the two words that sound like sounds (like *buzz* or *flop*) in the poem **"I'm Sorry"** (p. 46)?

Poof!
Shazam!

PowerPack 6: Alliteration

When poets use alliteration, they repeat initial consonants in a row for effect.
In **"New Idea"** (p. 52), find the many words that begin with W or S.
In **"Bouncing Along the Trail"** (p. 53), find the words that begin with J or W.
In **"A Weekend Away"** (p. 54), find the pairs of words that begin with B, M, F, W, or H.

"New Idea" (W or S): Wandering, woods, Wondering, why, we're, Whistling, Welcoming; Sal, stays, scratches, scruff, stick, Sky, sun
"Bouncing Along the Trail" (J or W): Jesse, jokes, Just; walking, with, wonder, why, want
"A Weekend Away" (B, M, F, W, or H): built big; melted marshmallows; five fish; wild weekend; holiday heaven

114

PowerPack 7: Vivid vocabulary

Poets use vivid words to paint a picture with their poems. What vivid words do you see in each of these poems?
"Book Hound" (p. 60)
"Reading" (p. 61)
"Writing" (p. 62)

"Writing": imagination, hopping
"Reading": giggles, discover, mistake
nudges, yips
"Book Hound": twinkling, wriggles,

PowerPack 8: Adjectives

Poets use descriptive words or adjectives to add details to the cats in these poems. What are some of those descriptive words?
"Lost and Found" (p. 68)
"Sick" (p. 70)

"Sick": strange, sluggish, tired
"Lost and Found": curious, gray, sad

PowerPack 9: Quotation marks

Find the quotation marks (" ") in these poems:
"Trust" (p. 76)
"Our Vet Speaks Cat" (p. 77)
"Good News" (p. 78)

"Good News"
"Kristy's cat is sick."
"That's part of having a pet."
"Is Kristy's cat going to die?"
"Let's see what they hear from the vet."
"What did you say?
That's great! That's crazy!"
"Kristy's cat isn't sick?"
"She's just having babies!"

"Our Vet Speaks Cat"
"Cat"; "Vet"; "Hmm, hummm"; "rrrrr,
purrrrr"; "Pet"
"Trust"
"I'll help"; "You'll be fine"

PowerPack 10: Number words

Sometimes poets use number words in poems for special emphasis. Find the number words in these poems:
"I Need Help!" (p. 85)
"Helping Our Neighbors" (p. 86)

And seven dogs have me!
I have seven dogs.
There is one dog
I walk seven dogs
"Helping Our Neighbors":
"I Need Help!": Three of them... a trio

PowerPack 11: Capitalization & proper nouns

Find the words that begin with capital letters in these poems:
"I Had to Get a Shot at the Doctor's" (p. 92)
(there's only one!)
"My Newest Friend" (p. 93)
"Homes" (p. 94)
Sometimes a capitalized word is the first word in the line, a name, or an abbreviation, and sometimes a word is capitalized just for emphasis.

She, I, Would, YES, When, Amy's, Her, One
"Homes": We're, Sweetness, We, Today, Amy,
Daniel, Amy, We, Maybe
Dane, G.D., North, Dakota, He, Kristy,
Avenue, Park, James, Boston, Bossy, Great,
"My Newest Friend": Last, Washington,
"I Had to Get a Shot at the Doctor's": James

PowerPack 12: Rebus Poems

You can be really creative and use pictures along with words to build a poem. Using pictures to suggest words is called creating a **rebus**. Which words are represented with pictures in these poems?
"Kitten" (p. 100)
"Surprise" (p. 101)
"Pet Crazy" (p. 102)

frog, turtles
"Pet Crazy": kitten or cat, one, up, dog,
kitten or cat
"Surprise": 9:00, knocks, door, box, eyes,
run
"Kitten": kitten or cat, laugh or happy, tail,

ABOUT THE POETS

Biographical information, photos, and lists of some of the books by our contributing poets can be found at PomeloBooks.com. Most poets have their own websites, too, where you can find their contact info, news about their books, and even links to their blogs. The first dozen poets listed here wrote the anchor poems in this book. Several of these poems appeared first in The Poetry Friday Anthology series. Janet Wong wrote all poems in the voices of Ben, Daniel, and Kristy. For more information, go to PomeloBooks.com.

Kristy Dempsey
KristyDempsey.com
Kristy Dempsey is the author of *Me with You, Mini Racer, Surfer Chick, A Dance Like Starlight, Superhero Instruction Manual,* and more. She grew up in South Carolina, but now works as a teacher at The American School of Belo Horizonte in Brazil. Dogs are her favorite, but through the years a couple of cats named Rascal and Minnie have curled their way into her heart as well.

Helen Frost
HelenFrost.net
Helen Frost is the award-winning author of *Monarch and Milkweed, Step Gently Out, Applesauce Weather, Among a Thousand Fireflies, Diamond Willow, Hidden, Salt,* and other poetry picture books and novels in verse. She is one of ten children and enjoys raising and releasing monarch butterflies.

Janice Harrington
JaniceHarrington.com
Janice Harrington grew up in rural Alabama and Nebraska and is the author of the poetic picture books *The Chicken-Chasing Queen of Lamar County* and *Going North,* and *Catching a Storyfish,* a novel in verse. She is a former librarian and now teaches creative writing at the University of Illinois. Her family had many pets; her favorite was a wonderful mutt named Nipper.

Eric Ode
EricOde.com
Eric Ode (pronounced OH-dee) is an author, poet, singer, and songwriter. He lives in Washington State and has written books of poetry about the Pacific Coast, pirates, cowboys, and wetlands. When Eric was an elementary teacher, he had many classroom pets including painted turtles, red-bellied newts, and a very friendly rat named Crockett.

Laura Shovan
LauraShovan.com
Laura Shovan grew up in a family with New York, British, and Thai influences. She published her first story in second grade and went on to teach high school and work as a journalist. Her novel in verse, *The Last Fifth Grade of Emerson Elementary,* has won multiple awards. Her family has lost a beloved cat, Nutmeg, just like in the poem she wrote.

Elizabeth Steinglass
ElizabethSteinglass.com
Elizabeth Steinglass lives in Washington, DC with her husband, two children, and her sleepy cat, Scout. Her poetry has appeared in *Ladybug* and *High Five* magazines and in *The Poetry Friday Anthology for Celebrations.* Her book *Soccer Nonsense* is forthcoming from Boyds Mills Press.

Eileen Spinelli

EileenSpinelli.com

Eileen Spinelli grew up in Pennsylvania and began writing at the age of six when her father gave her an old manual typewriter. She has written more than 70 children's books and poetry collections, including *Peace Week in Miss Fox's Class, Another Day as Emily, Silly Tilly, Where I Live, Polar Bear Arctic Hare,* and *Somebody Loves You, Mr. Hatch.* She and her husband raise monarch butterflies.

Don Tate

DonTate.com

Don Tate is an author and artist and founding member of The Brown Bookshelf blog dedicated to highlighting books by African American writers. He grew up in Iowa and now lives in Texas. He has illustrated more than 50 books for children and also authored several picture books, including *Poet: The Remarkable Story of George Moses Horton.*

Padma Venkatraman

PadmaVenkatraman.com

Padma Venkatraman is an American author who was born in India and lives in Rhode Island. She is an oceanographer and scientist and has authored many science articles for children and adults. She is also a poet and writer of several award-winning books for young people, including *Climbing the Stairs, A Time to Dance,* and *Island's End.*

April Halprin Wayland

AprilWayland.com

April Halprin Wayland grew up in California and has been a nanny for a TV star, traveled through Europe, and worked on a farm. Now she writes for young people, plays violin, and teaches writing. She has authored a novel in verse and several picture books, including *More Than Enough: A Passover Story.* Her beloved dog Eli is the heart of her family.

Tamera Will Wissinger

TameraWillWissinger.com

Tamera Will Wissinger grew up in Iowa in a family that loved going fishing, which was the focus of her first poetry book, *Gone Fishing.* Now she lives near the water in Florida where she loves boating and outdoor activities. Her book *Gone Camping* continues those outdoor adventures. Tamera once had a small cat that was a ball retriever.

Carole Boston Weatherford

CBWeatherford.com

Carole Boston Weatherford grew up in Baltimore, Maryland and is a Professor of English at Fayetteville State University in North Carolina. Her award-winning work celebrates African American experiences and honors many forgotten heroes in books such as *First Pooch: The Obamas Pick a Pet, Freedom in Congo Square,* and *Jazz Baby,* among many, many others. Over the years, she has shared a home with beagles Lucky, Snoopy, Hendrix, and Gigi.

Janet Wong

JanetWong.com

Janet Wong is the author of thirty books, including the poetry collections *Knock on Wood: Poems about Superstitions* and *Twist: Yoga Poems,* and a verse novel, *Minn and Jake,* filled with pet fish and lizards. Her favorite pet ever was a Norwegian Buhund named Nissa.

POEM CREDITS

POET INDEX

TITLE INDEX

ABOUT THE CREATORS

Sylvia M. Vardell is Professor at Texas Woman's University and teaches children's and young adult literature. She has published five books on literature, plus more than 25 book chapters and 100 journal articles. Her current work focuses on poetry for young people, including a blog, *Poetry for Children*. Her favorite pets are dogs and she's had three of them (Luther, Yenta, and Caesar, each for many years), as well as Leonardo the tortoise, and Pecky the parakeet.

Janet S. Wong is a graduate of Yale Law School and a former lawyer who became a children's poet. Her work has been featured on *The Oprah Winfrey Show* and other shows. She is the author of 30 books for children on identity, chess, creative recycling, yoga, and more. She has had dozens of pets, including birds, fish, a frog, hamsters, lizards, turtles, a cat, and favorite dogs named Bernadette, Coco, Nissa, and Angel.

Together, Vardell and Wong are the creative forces behind *The Poetry Friday Anthology* and *Poetry Friday Power Book* series.

Franzi Paetzold is a freelance illustrator from Germany. As a globetrotter and former social worker, she spent much of her life traveling the world, studying and working abroad. In between work and plane rides, she started publishing her drawings online and taking on small assignments. She now illustrates full time, and lives with a friend and two friendly cats in Berlin. Her illustrations can be found at franzidraws.com.

ABOUT THE POETRY FRIDAY ANTHOLOGY® SERIES

In *The Poetry Friday Anthology* series, we have created a unique resource that blends original poetry by today's best and brightest poets writing for young people and teaching strategies that make it easy to introduce poetry, engage readers, and reinforce learning objectives. The organizational features of each book make it quick and easy to find, share, and teach poetry at multiple levels and across the curriculum. We strive to balance communicating the joy and playfulness of poetry with learning important concepts and skills.

HERE WE GO: A POETRY FRIDAY POWER BOOK

Can kids change the world? How about starting with a walkathon, a food drive, and a school garden? *(a CBC Hot Off the Press selection)*

YOU JUST WAIT: A POETRY FRIDAY POWER BOOK

This book is for teens and tweens who love soccer, basketball, and movies! *(an NCTE Poetry Notable)*

Titles in this **Poetry Friday Power Book** read-and-write series feature 12 PowerPack sets that combine 1) diverse anchor poems; 2) new original response poems and mentor poems; 3) creative and inspiring PowerPlay prewriting activities; and 4) engaging skill-based Power2You writing prompts

THE POETRY FRIDAY ANTHOLOGY FOR K-5
(TEACHER EDITION)

218 poems by 76 poets about school, pets, favorite sports, food, friends, free time, vacation, books, and more, with *Take 5!* mini-lessons for each poem

THE POETRY FRIDAY ANTHOLOGY FOR MIDDLE SCHOOL
(TEACHER EDITION)

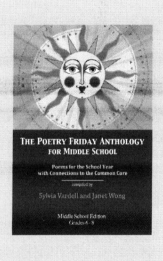

110 poems by 71 poets about new schools, coping with family, playing soccer, and texting friends, with *Take 5!* mini-lessons for every poem *(an NCTE Poetry Notable)*

THE POETRY FRIDAY ANTHOLOGY FOR CELEBRATIONS
(TEACHER EDITION AND STUDENT EDITION)

156 poems by 115 poets in English and Spanish about celebrations from Halloween to National Pizza Week to National Bike Month and more *(an ILA-CL/R Notable Book for a Global Society)*

THE POETRY FRIDAY ANTHOLOGY FOR SCIENCE
(THE POETRY OF SCIENCE - STUDENT EDITION)

200+ science poems on a wide variety of topics, including engineering, technology, and inventions *(NSTA Recommends)*

For more information about *The Poetry Friday Anthology* series, please visit **PomeloBooks.com**.

121

YOUR OWN
PERSONAL POWER PAGES

DOODLE SKETCH DRAW LIST WRITE
BRAINSTORM HEARTSTORM

YOUR OWN
PERSONAL POWER PAGES

DOODLE SKETCH DRAW LIST WRITE
BRAINSTORM HEARTSTORM